Other Titl

Konglanjo

(Spears of Love without Ill-fortune)
and
Letters to Ethiopia with Some

Random Poems

Bongasu Tanla Kishani

Langaa Research & Publishing CIG
Mankon, Bamenda

Publisher:
Langaa RPCIG
Langaa Research & Publishing Common Initiative Group
P.O. Box 902 Mankon
Bamenda
North West Region
Cameroon
Langaagrp@gmail.com
www.langaa-rpcig.net

Distributed outside N. America by African Books Collective
orders@africanbookscollective.com
www.africanbookscollective.com

Distributed in N. America by Michigan State University Press
msupress@msu.edu
www.msupress.msu.edu

ISBN: 9956-616-04-4

DISCLAIMER

The names, characters, places and incidents in this book are either the product of the author's imagination or are used fictitiously. Accordingly, any resemblance to actual persons, living or dead, events, or locales is entirely one of incredible coincidence.

Content

Koŋlànjò
(Spears Of Love Without Ill-fortune)

Letters To Ethiopia

In Memory of Our Father,

Moósér Kíshaàne Yeèkpu Kòŋnyùy,

(1902 – 1980)

An Eminent Philosopher and Scientific Mind,

All Told, Worthy of Emulation.

Foreword to the First Edition

The first day I fetched my heaps of papers and put this collection of poems together, it soon occurred to me that I had already been on the job since 1965. That was in 1984. Ever since the match between myself, the author, and the publishers has continued more regularly, without the public referee blowing the whistle for either half-time or for a score. All I have experienced has been a series of offside plays.

Thus aware of a public desire to assist at a fair match which really becomes interesting to participate in when one plays a part well or in a way that obliges the referee to decide the winner on merits, the University of Yaounde went ahead to provide the public with the publication of this collection of poems. Though most of the titles of the poems remain the same like people we know when they are young and when they become old with the same names, some of them have undergone changes like titled ladies and gentlemen. There are, however, some obvious disparities between earlier publications and the versions as they appear in this collection.

The reason is simple. Perfection is a handmaid of imperfection in every human experience, especially as my own endeavours here can testify. This is far from suggesting that I am not grateful to particular reviews and publishers like *Abbia, Cameroon Cultural Review, Présence Africaine, Cultural Review of the Negro World, The African Theatre Review, New Horizons, Loquitur, Cardinal Henry Newman's Review, St. Augustine's Review*, etc, in which some of my poems have appeared. On the contrary, this is an opportunity I am seizing to pay them tribute and to thank them for allowing me to publish, though in modified forms, earlier versions of my poems. I do not hesitate to encourage them to continue publishing the works of unpublished authors, especially the best, irrespective of personal or ethnocentric tastes.

For the rest, I have provided a glossary to explain some of the words, with a Cameroonian or a Lăm Nso' background in order to facilitate some of the problems within my own creative activity. Whatever the reader's taste, no matter his or her origin, this poetry is based on the lives of my own lived human experiences. As such, it refuses to be dismissed with the sheer catalogue of likeness at the expense of unlikeness.

This poetry aims at new perspectives, one of which is to reflect, point to and translate the life of tone languages without becoming an oral exercise.

Bongasu Tanla Kishani (1988)

Foreword to the Second Edition

The extent to which the poems we write, survive as a reflection of 'tone languages without exerting an oral exercise,' is a matter for our readers to judge for themselves. In the course of more than twenty years since the publication of the first collection of these poems, much has happened and still continues to happen. I soon became more aware of the necessity of writing poetry not only in English, but also in Lăm Nso' in order to benefit from the virtues of oraurality and promote literacy within African cultures. For, not only "Like us, nobody can ever shave your head in your absence," but also to address both national and international issues in and with poetry, an African / Cameroonian poet that I am, equally needs to rethink a certain strategy of action for the development of his or her African language. A few of Cameroon's languages like Lăm Nso' have since the 1970s been gradually taking their first steps and carving out their own eventual seats among the world's literate languages. This explains why I have not only embraced educating myself in literate Lăm Nso' as an instrument of cultural development, but have also been making use of English as another means of confirming an African presence in the contemporary global cultures. In fact, to judge from such wonders of *techno-oraurality* like microphones, telephones, radio, television and computers, *oraurality* today all over the world has a plurality of literate bedfellows with whom it shares cultural legacies and whose diversity depends on the simultaneous collaboration between the human senses and the mind.

The present edition reflects some of the major progressive landmarks that have been occurring in the African poetic arena since I first set my hands into poetry back in 1965. African languages, especially those in the Southern part of the Sahara Desert, whose tonal nature was then more or less disputably limited to experts, have almost definitely been acknowledged as tonal languages.

More specifically, both literate and "oral traditions" everywhere have now distinguished themselves as cultural legacies more on the basis of mutually complementary rather than rival partners. Yet, more than ever before, a new turning point that defines itself as 'the electronic era' is consistently emerging in full swing. It works to clarify certain scientific choices and offer a more legitimate functional basis for questioning such paradigms as those of "orality" and "orature" that tend to emphasize only the partial role the mouth plays instead of the concretely functional role the mouth and ears play together as all the senses work hand in hand with and under the guidance of the mind. Consequently, our research has enabled us to opt for the paradigm of oraurality in contrast with the paradigms of 'orality and orature.' Our perceptive choice for the oraural aims at setting research a step ahead. For, it presents the oraural within the world of the senses as the *in vivo* collaborative functioning of the ears and the mouth to concretely produce and receive ephemeral language units and thus readily avoid the ambiguity that accrues from similar but not identical medical uses of the term, 'oral' for example.

With this in mind, I would first like to pay homage to late Dr. Bate Besong whose literary works will ever keep him alive, in spite of his tragic death in a car accident on Thursday 8th of March 2007, along with Kwasen Gwangwa'a and Hilarius Ngwa Ambe. Bate Besong in 1978 comfortably surprised me by drawing the attention of the readership to my poetry with an article in *Cameroon Tribune*. Ever since and until his catastrophic death, he continuously kept pace with the evolution of my poetry. I later learned that he had presented copies of *Konglanjo (Spears of Love without Ill-fortune)* (1988) to *The Association of Nigerian Authors (ANA)* for an award in 1990. Secondly, I would also like to pay tribute still in memoriam to late Prof. Siga Asanga. His sudden death here in Yawunde has since left me tongue-tied and unable to overcome my shock and find the apposite words to express my bewilderment. He was the first to write a review of an earlier publication of *Konglanjo (Spears of Love without Ill-fortune)* in 1982. In paying him this tribute, I also wish to express my gratitude to the entire Board of Directors and Editors of *ABBIA, Cameroon Cultural Review,* who, under Bernard Nso'kika Fonlon (1924-1986), editor in-chief, had first published my poetry in 1969 as Neil Alden Armstrong, the American astronaut and the first to walk on the moon, made history. Finally, I would still like to thank Mr. Alfred Vensu for proofreading the glossary of Lăm Nso' terms as well as all those who have in any other way directly or indirectly contributed to the entire publication of these poems.

Bongasu Tanla Kishani (2009)

KOŊLÀNJÒ

(SPEARS OF LOVE WITHOUT ILL-FORTUNE)

A) CALLING

1.

There,
where fields pasture our cattle,
grow our corn,
saár- millet,
kikéŋ - peace plant;
where forests that nest our birds and shrines
from sunburns and sun-strokes;
where drums blend breathings
of festal *Mànjòŋ* gongs
inviting, summoning
for the Fon's Solemn Call
to a sacrificial grove with palm-wine,
camwood, baskets of black fowls, a tethered goat,
corn-loaves and bags of unmasked capsules of kola nut,
we stitch'd and webb'd
all the edges of smiles, to season
the smouldering log fires of incense
invoking mighty *Ŋgaà-Mbóm*.

There,
heralds emerge,
struggling and nagging like hunting dogs
with the unposted omens of their incoming!
On the one hand, they display a new coin of faith,
on the other, a new arm-quiver of knowledge!
And in fright, we smoulder all our tears of persuasion
in a riotous bid of transmitting relics and tracks of all
we had wrought and reaped and conveyed
throughout our days of fortune and misfortune.
But in vain –
In vain do our streams of blood
replace streams of our victim's blood
in a bid to entice you, O Heralds,
from your resolute way!

3

In vain, O Heralds,
do you fail to drink
from our medicine-pots of faith and knowledge.
In vain do you forget to wave our Fon's distaff
in token of your calling,
in token of our coming
to share in the benevolence
of your new oracle.

2.

Heralds!
Whatever news you bear,
we still cleave to the best –
inquirers on a pilgrim's staggered step.
Echoes of our legends
brood on men's words,
soothe men's woes,
but echoes of river falls
spill rivers of hope
springs of joyful hope -
a spirited push to a pilgrim's end.
We are pilgrims from a cradle
in our ancestor's land
with shoulders laden with palm-wine calabashes,
palm-oil, palm-bags of groundnuts,
palm-kernels and baskets of towering cocks
that sing the morning or evening hymns
at each majestic stone – now
becoming a mushroom home
with florid ornaments of blood.

Heralds all,
We cling to the shrine
Of our Védo'ó's father's father's ....father.
For,
on this stone lay the first victim,
from this stone ran the first trickle,

to this stone we return,
around this stone we flirt with the gods.
Heralds!
Here,
a rustling hush
c-r-a-c-k-l-e-s
to reign beyond those palm-fronds
of muffled voices of coughs and steps on dry leaves.

Here,
benumbed with atonement and thanksgiving
our setting sun buries still
the voice of a cock;
the morning guest welcomes
black fowls, tethered goats
a loaf, kola nuts and camwood.

Here Ŋgaà-Mbóm smiles!
And from there we till, we sow, we crop
seasons of *Mànjòŋ, Coŋ* and *Cíkàŋ* – drummings
we oil and salt with ingredients of xylophone notes
as we smile too,
and mount years of vigils,
weeping over our dead,
attending to our sick,
and rejoicing over our new born.

3.

Ŋgaà-Mbóm! May we keep to the spoors of faith!
May evil omens pass and go their solitary ways
and leave our children and lands in peace!
If they come in the winds,
let them fly above the highest clouds!
If they spring from our soils,
let them be washed away by rain and stream!
If they fall from the heavens,

let thunder and lightening consume them!
And should they suddenly appear
in our lands as if from nowhere,
may you enlighten our innermost spider-college
of medicine-pot boilers to determine
whether they were brought by man and not by a god!

Ŋgaà-Mbóm!
Behold the prayerful spears of rain we keep showering
on these nubile shrines – the anvil of your name!
Shrines of sure choice, not of our making,
to crop and awaken life
for the strong, the sick, the dead
and those being born into life and death.
For, whither you smile
we chew and eschew the spittle that moistens
our sacred moulds of reconciliation at every cross-road.
Our door-step log drips
the unblemished blood of a rightly chosen victim.
We pour libations of memorial mites of dreams
and plant anointed trees out of mighty hopes.
Horizons wane our fears with a myriad of uninvited songs
we improvise on ancestral octaves to grace
a *kwí'fòn*-drumming of prayers and vows
beyond those sacred palm-fronds
where our seers labour best and sound.

Ŋgaà-Mbóm!
May we espy and cry shame on whoever mocks you!
May our foes be ignorant of our woes!
May we sow and reap in folds of eight hundreds!
May we grow strong!
May we prosper!
May the good-hearted live long
within the rhythms of the seasons!
May the evil-doer and the warrior miss their way!
May we build on the epitaphs of ancestral feats!
May the realms of our households never dwindle under
our feet!

May our offspring hunt for game of therapeutic inspirations
from the upper stream-forests to the lower stream-forests;
from the hillside forests on our left
to the hillside forests on our right!
May echoes of our lineage name toll and spread
beyond years issuing from the echoes and rhythms
of these festal *Mànjòŋ* gongs! *Kù-ŋgu-ŋguŋ!*

Ŋgaà-Mbóm!
Inspire our furrowed fruits!
Inspire the soils
whither our proverbial lineage head first ventured
to woo, crown, govern and nurse our years
with royal tools and stools now frizzled and freshened
with due slaps of stately usage and libations.

Ŋgaà-Mbóm!
We pray Thee to inspire our *Tíŋekárí* Stock,
to order, feed and enrich our necromancy as of yore!
Inspire this revolving stock to scan the silence of our days
still girded and yoked
to the very navel of mirroring generations!
Inspire us through these leafy cards of *Mfuu*!
Inspire us through the oracular spider's gait!
Inspire us through this porcupine's quill!
Inspire us through this *kilún* egg-plants and egg-fruits –
chosen and cropped unbroken from nature's best!
Inspire us through the dicta of these kola nut parings
to scratch out witch bites and sight the parasite,
jiggering within our family-trees
and scan the remnant isthmuses,
still stemming from our florid homes!

Ngaà-Mbóm!
Let our forgotten words still breathe forth
and whisper our needs!
Let these siphon-hands
we clap, couple and mouth-cup, decant
fortune-designs you hand-write

7

on the unfretted leaves of our age!
Let the eyeless bear and follow the eye-owner's counsels
for the welfare of our peoples and lands!
Let the weathering days never disdain and break out
from the hands of the rain-maker!
Let our medicine pots duly reward
the innocent, the thief and the witch!
May our spears of good omens never return unstained!

But Ŋgaà-Mbóm, nay!
Within your seasons we give birth to all -
the good-hearted and the evil-doer,
the wise and the foolish,
the thief and the witch!

Ŋgaà-Mbóm, again avert it!
Our times now burn
with uncontrollable flames,
driving us headlong to embrace the unknown
with our blameless arms.

Ŋgaà-Mbóm!
Alone, You know it nameless to our ears,
shapeless before our eyes
and untrodden from ancestral days!
Be it death, let it take us and spare our children
and no longer sustain us thus spell-bound
within this sacred labyrinth of seers and non-seers!
But if it be life, why should she awe us still-
already usurped and snatched as we are
from rival eras before and after our footfalls?
Why should she now crown us suddenly
with frailty's best, enabling volunteers to sing
the songs of our own making and woes?

Ŋgaà-Mbóm! Once more avert it!
Let it go back through this spittle of disdain
as it came, (*spitting*) tà!

Ŋgaà-Mbóm! Thou who gave us to our times and lands, receive our supplications from within this grove ever inflated by the silence of your presence!

4.

For, here as in days of old,
wind, storm and thunder,
bird, tadpole and termite,
worm, stream and stone
eavesdrop
and woods and springs sprout,
and resilient snakes freely move and canvass
from ant-hill to ant-hill, fondly mirroring
garlands of nature's cowries
and a fair flair for the evil-doer and the peace-maker,
while, driven into ecstatic spells, we welcome
every incoming season with flutes, drums and gongs thus

> *Faáyí tóŋ loŋ a ji feè!   The Faáy sounds the flute feè!*
> *Faáyí tóŋ loŋ a ji feè fee!   The Faáy sounds the flute feè fee!*
> *Faáyí kum ncùm á ji tìndíŋ!   The Faáy sounds the drum tìndíŋ!*
> *Faáyí kum ncùm á ji tìndíŋ tindiŋ!   The Faáy sounds the drum*
> *   tìndíŋ tindiŋ!*
> *Faáyí kum ŋgèm a ji kìŋgìŋ!   The Faáy sounds the gongs*
> *   kìŋgìŋ!*
> *Faáyí kum ŋgèm a ji kìŋgìŋ, kiŋgiŋ!   The Faáy sounds the gongs*
> *   Kìŋgìŋ kiŋgiŋ!*
> *Faáyí kum ŋgù' á ji kùŋgùŋ!   The Faáy sounds the wooden-gongs*
> *   kùŋgùŋ!*
> *Faáyí kum ŋgù' á ji kùŋgùŋ!   Kuŋguŋ!   The Faáy sounds*
> *   the wooden-gongs kùŋgùŋ!   Kuŋguŋ!*

> *Kù-ŋgùŋ!   Kù-ŋgu-ŋguŋ!   Kù-ŋgùŋ!   Ku-ŋguŋ!*
> *Kì-ŋgìŋ!   Kì-ŋgi-ŋgiŋ!   Kì-ŋgìŋ!   Ki-ŋgiŋ!*
> *Tì-ŋdìŋ!   Tì-ndi-ndiŋ!   Tì-ndìŋ!   Ti-ndiŋ!*
> *Kù-ŋgu-ŋguŋ!   Kù-ŋgùŋ!   Kù!   Kù-ŋgùŋ!*
> *Kù-ŋgu-ŋguŋ!   Kù-ŋgùŋ Kù!   Kù-ŋgùŋ!*

5.

Out from this ecstasy we journey still
on the spoors and echoes
of unforgotten proverbial names,
drumming anew the first ancestral ventures
of Lè' and Njíŋ, a life-begotten couple,
once dementedly driven and tossed
through rival winds of dissension and hunger
away from all
the eye can see
the ear can hear
the nose can smell
the hand can touch
and thus left to eke out their last drops of hope
uprooting fear from the eye
whispering hope into the ear
blowing life through the nostrils
and planting courage in the hand
in a bid to coddle our way.

On the one day
we harvest crops plucked from nature's sowing
and name it, *Kaáví*, a harvesting Day!

On the one day
we enkindle fire and ignite its clamorous voice
and name it, *Rəávəy*, a fire-heralding Day!

On the one day
we soothe our log fires to smoulder while we still forage
and name it Kiloòvəy, a fire-nursing Day!

On the one day
with naked ears we struggle through wind and storm
until we become rivals to their laws
and name it, *Nsəərí*, a law-deafening Day!

On the one day
worn out we snail-pace to the rhythms of our footfalls
and name it, *Geegee,* a nerve-and-muscle-drooping Day!

On the one day
we stock seeds into barns
and proclaim the dusk of the dry-season
with the harvest of the last *kishò'*-plant reddening
and ripening with the predictions of the first homestead
rains
and name it, *Ŋgòylùm,* an all-round storing Day!

On the one day
we sow, sell and sheathe in harmony with the dictions
and dictations of a diviner-egg
and name it, *Wáylùn,* an egg-pod planting Day!

On the one day
we crown with a solemn sacrifice
to ride peacefully over our days
and rid our revolving stock of ill-omens
amidst drummings of a tattered Ŋwéròŋ,
usurped from revolving homesteads
and kept with its germ-talent of inventions and laws,
knitting our Fons and peoples into a single breathing-web
of unity
and name it, *Ntàŋrìn,* a reconciliation Day,
A *Ŋgùmba-Ŋwéròŋ-and Kwí'fòn Day!*

6.

Wà'bìn!
Youth of every land! Youth of every time!
as if with the trappings of our royal wine-calabashes
we cease not to harness and oil your pumpkin-jaws!
As if invited by a drummer's voice
we dance our dance of age to the sway of time's tunes

to open the footpath of your dance
and spellbind you to rattle the cymbals of your fashion
and live the way our fuzzy forerunners live!
Not in vain do we keep unfolding these secret rites
of the first spider-legged weeks we store still
with seasons of sun shines and rainfalls on those ledges of
years
whence we stem like a stream from its source;
whence we stem like corn-grains from corn-cobs;
whence we stem like forests from the soil;
whence we stem like a knife from its handle;
whence we stem like rain from the sky;
whence we stem like a road from a homestead;
whence we breathe forth like life from our veins!
Not in vain do we bequeen
and name our daughter, Ntàŋ,
in commemoration,
yes, in commemoration
of the first *hammock-bridge*
of our first crossing away from parental homesteads!

Listen! Wà'bìn listen!
Listen to every voice blowing centuries of dreams into
your ears!
Wà'bìn!
Listen to them saying from within this caravan of streams
that we are more than a start, more than an end!
Let us name, write down and praise
the first of things, peoples, lands and times,
known and unknown,
born and still to be born,
harvested or planted:
things first spoken but never done;
things first done but never spoken;
a wedlock of webs of silence and words,
as the cobweb-spinners of our times!

The first of things and peoples
to have overridden and despoiled
the first lands for our revolving stock,
Oh *Tíŋekárí Wà 'bìn*!
The first to have driven all like a river
into the ebb and flow of new names!
The first to have unfolded the first dreams
under the first roofs
away from the first rainfalls and sun shines
that tended our first crops!
The first to have begotten and sung the first lullabies
to our first children within our first homesteads!
The first to have invented
the first set of tally-sticks to record
the first southerly moon rise
we proverbially capture to name
the first Ŋwéròŋ drummings
and gong-sounds behind the first palm-fronds,
inviting and inviting *Ŋgírì* drummings
into a relay-race of vigilance
throughout seasons of fortune and misfortune!
The first to have sprinkled this rounded stone of sacrifice
with the first camwood-powder
and planted the first perennial Kikéŋ!
The first elephant that provided the first tusk-sound
for the first *Taàmànjòŋ*
who rallied the first Mànjòŋ to crown
the first *Lion* to have soothed
his noble feet on the first leopard-skin!

The first to have evaluated the first of nature's cowries!
The first to have inaugurated the first market
with the first anointed fig-tree!
The first to have plucked the first calabash
for the first libations!
The first to have worn the first tattoos
with the first hairstyles!

The first to have carved
the first wooden doors and hearth-posts!
The first to have boiled
the first medicine-plants in the first medicine-pots!
The first to have translated
the first bidding of an earth-spider!
The first to have sent and deciphered
the first message with porcupine-quills!
The first to have harvested the first voice
of kola nut parings!
The first to have recalled the first rains
after the first rainlessness!
The first to have spied the approach
of the first locust of destruction!
The first to have begotten, sealed and handed on
these eponyms still held inviolate
within the breathings of a sacred lineage-*mèŋkfɔ́m*!
The first to have worn
the first head-gear, neckwear and girdle
with their corresponding staffs of nobility!

The first to have inaugurated the *Ŋgàŋ* mask-dance
with the first xylophones!
The first to have invented
every Mànjòŋ and Coŋ family-dances
with the first drums and cymbals!
The first to have begotten Thee, Oh Cíkàŋ,
the unrivalled offspring of Bíikan!
The first to have endured
the first whips of a lineage invitation
to couple with the first lineage lady
and put on the first lineage head-gear!
The first to have paid
the first homage to a maternal homestead!
The first to have heard
the first stir of our rising suns, *Oh Tíŋekárí*!
The first, the first...Mothers and Fathers
of our inventions and laws

an age of ages ago,
Oh Wà'bìn,
Youth of every land and time!

Kì-ŋgi-ŋgiŋ! Kì-ŋgìŋ! Ki-ŋgiŋ!
Kù-ŋgu-ŋguŋ! Kù-ŋgùŋ! Ku-ŋguŋ!

7.

Ŋgaà-Mbóm!
In this grove we breathe the same breath of unison with
the Fon!
Let these trickles
of our rams and cocks not miss their way!
We pray for peace, good harvesting and planting seasons!
Taàwòŋ take!
May your good-natured gongs
ever sound the approach of seasons!
Yeèwòŋ take!
May your stately hoe
ever open our farms to new seasons!
Taànto' take!
Let this wine strengthen you to guide every incomer!
Ŋgàywìr take!
Let this bloodstained feather bear testimony to our sacrifice!
Tav-Mfu' take!
Let the sound of your drums, gongs
and tusks assemble the Fon's peoples!
Taàŋgwà' take!
Let our Mbokàm game yield
to the wishes of your spears and dogs!
Taàmànjòŋ take!
May you continue to lead our Mànjòŋ standard bearers!
Taàwónlè take!
May you open the ears of young folks to new things!
Yeèwónlè take!
May you blow life into the children you name!

You present beneath our feet!
You breathing around our feet,
be you good or bad, mad or sad,
be you alive or dead, dying or being born,
may you drink from this medicine-pot of unity,
rub this camwood of nobility,
lick up this oil of harmony,
season your ways with this salt of truth
and share this kola nut of laws and friendship,
be it, big or small, kolaly bitter or sweet!

You present beneath our feet,
you breathing around our feet,
let no fears woo and turn you
away from your earthen mites of mights and rights!
You, fathers of the lands! You, mothers of the lands!
Youth of every land and time!
Kwí'fòn-custodians in our new springs!
If you sink, sink with kwí'fòn on your shoulders!
If you rise, let the kwí'fòn drummings open your steps!
We are more than a start! We are more than the end!
Yet, we now burst into the tears of our times,
invaded, twisted and planted to grow roots of fears!
Rooted fears that strip every oasis of our knowledge!
Rooted fears that presage a new disease without elixir!
Rooted fears that drill their tongue-twisters into our lives!

Nay! Ŋgaà-Mbóm!
Once more take and pour fortune on our lands!
Let one that goes, go with the peaceful steps of fortune!
Let one that now comes, come
with the fortune-tidings of a good harvesting season!
Let these trickles sprinkle fortune on our lands and times!

Kù-ŋgu-ŋguŋ! Kù-ŋgùŋ! Ku-ŋguŋ!
Kì-ŋgi-ŋgiŋ! Kì-ŋgìŋ! Ki-ŋgiŋ!
Kù-ŋgu-ŋguŋ! Kù-ŋgùŋ! Ku-ŋguŋ!
Kù-ŋgu-ŋguŋ! Kù-ŋgùŋ! Ku!

16

Today,
we inaugurate to proclaim a new harvesting season for
seeds!
Today,
we inaugurate to proclaim a new planting season for crops!
News,
we shell like kola nuts out of pods!
News,
we pluck like unripe fruits from podding winds!

Kù-ŋgu-ŋguŋ! Kù-ŋgùŋ! Ku! (silence) Kù-ŋgùŋ!

Children will be tilled like fertile lands
and wooed to weather on with varying tonsures!
Showers of blood will drive off showers of rain
to retreat into their sky-like homes with their blessings!
Pumpkin-plants will withdraw their gourd-like pods!
Lands will exhale and exchange names for gold and weep
like the heavens without consolation!
News, planted to grow in clumps within farms of winds!
There is a skin-disease, grafted somewhere to spread
and infect new incoming winds!
Bags of fertility sewn up unopened like a raffia wedding
bag,
no longer bear new medicine-plants for our weathering
days!

Kù-ŋgu-ŋguŋ! Kù-ŋùŋ Ku! (silence) Kù-ŋgùŋ!

A market message comes with the sealed orders
of the Fon and people together in unison
for a new planting and harvesting season!
A Market message breaks silence
with the single breath of seers and their mother-kwí'fòn
to exchange vigilance over all we had wrought
with the *ŋgírì* drummings for ages, but avoids blood
like You, O mighty Cíkàŋ,
Mountaineer of the indomitable Taàjò' mountains!

17

Kù-ŋgu-ŋgùŋ! Kù-ŋgùŋ! Kù!
Kù-ŋgùŋ! Ku-ŋguŋ! Kù-ŋgu-ŋguŋ! Ku!
Kù-ŋgu-ŋguŋ! Kù-ŋgùŋ! Kù-ŋgu-ŋguŋ!
Kù-ŋgùŋ! Ku!......... Kù-ŋgùŋ!

B) ANSWERING

8.

S: S: S:- D:- S: S: S:- D:- M:- S:- F:- :-
Shikùmkùm koó Shikumkum koó ji à wáa yu!
Shikùmkùm koó Shikumkum koó vibìŋ vée yuv!
Shikùmkùm koó Shikumkum koó vilùŋ vée nsay!

Bits of frictions battling.
Flights of efforts welcoming our lands.
Bits of exertions trapping heavenly doves!
Bits of exertions trapping earthly kites!
Nets of emanations expelling every yardstick,
we now break and heap behind our ears on soils,
embalmed and reddened with the camwood and red oil
of centuried layers of drummings and carvings!
Bits of exertions battling
with locust-caravans hastening into our lands!
Bits of exertions battling
with the *ntèm-ntém* disease of our kola trees!
Bits of exertions
we welcome through patches and wisps of scarecrows!
Bits of ill-wills reaping our lands,
defiling palm-fronds and boughs ornamenting godly
groves,
we pray you to fear a kwí'fòn earth-born disease!

For,
here where fields pasture our cattle,
grow our corn, saár-millet, kikéŋ-plant;

where forests that nest our birds and shrines
from sunburns and sun-strokes;
where drums blend breathings
of festal mànjòŋ gongs
inviting and inviting
for the Fon's solemn Call
to a sacrifice with palm-wine, camwood,
baskets of black fowls, a tethered goat
corn-loaves and bags of unmasked capsules of kola nut,
we stitch and weave webs bearing all the edges of smiles
to season the smouldering log fires of seasons
to invoke mighty Nyùy-Mbóm!

Here,
heralds emerged,
struggling and nagging like hunting dogs
with the unposted omens of their incoming!
On the one hand, they displayed a new coin of faith,
on the other hand, a new arm-quiver of knowledge,
defiling our *kwàŋkwàŋ* bows of knowledge
and in fright we smothered all our tears of persuasion
in a riotous bid of transmitting relics and tracks of all,
we had wrought and reaped and conveyed
throughout our days.

Heralds!
Whatever news you bear
we still cleave to the best –
inquirers on a pilgrim's staggered step,
within daily smiles of sunshine and rainfall.
At once *Nyùy-Mbóm* sends you!
At once *Nyùy-Mbóm* sends us!
We are pilgrims from a sacred cradle
in ancestral lands we still treasure and till!
Behold libations going before our feet,
proclaiming our coming to the departed beyond our feet!
Let our children lead the way!
Let our children continue within our footpaths!
Let our children repave trodden ways and open new paths!

Heralds!
Away from our hearing,
without our beckoning,
you bestirred the heavens of your coming!
By virtue of a dance
We discern the family-head, the noble...!
Springs that feed no creatures
dribble at their sources to a stop!
Behold us still imbued as ever,
with that same ancestral use and wont never to cross a hill
and return without a blood-stained spear!
Yet, without dancing you claim
the right of a family-head as a noble of our making!

Without stint your waters now spill into our door-space!
Yet see our benevolent gifts of oil and salt,
water, wine and kola nuts, carrots, groundnuts and sugar-
cane,
lest we be accused of failing to welcome a god!
Peacefully follow the very spoors of your coming,
appeased as wonted with our bloodless gifts
splendidly outgrowing godly places
within our cross-roads!
For, while waters flow and bridges keep the foothold
of our own crossings away from nurturing homesteads
our children grow and their dreams grope for realms
where fortresses fell and where fortresses rose
and age tethered age unleashed,
still yodelling title-names to rising homes,
with the pace of our age rising from fallen bones!

But here, our soils swell;
here, echoes in chorus hail from ancestral fame!
Here, we pray at cross-roads,
welcoming every peaceful incomer!
Let our children's children's children lead our way!
Let our children's children's children continue our way!

Heralds!
If you wish to defile the works of our making,
ask Taà-Mbóm who never fails us!
For, indiscriminately without any arms-hunting,
we receive smiles of sun shines
and the drumming-blessings of rainfalls
on our farms and homesteads!
Without any alms-hunting we live on
beyond the heavens, above a soil of no human making!

Heralds! To shame us is to incur not only yours, but ours!
Behold libations before, beneath and behind our footfalls!
Let our fathers endorse our beliefs
and our mothers endear them!
Let our sons consider and consolidate our courage!
Let our daughters propagate our hopes
and our ancestors quicken and sprout them!
May our bags of yesterday reveal their contents to-morrow,
if now we must march on like rivers with arms spreading
on the bigamous banks of ancestors and youth,
with our footholds of new clothings and monetary units
of new carvings and names!

Heralds! Those who inspire the way,
those who inquire a way, walk to work at best
within the wisdom steps of their inspiring inquiry!
Say no more about your incoming!
Like us, nobody can ever shave your head in your absence!
Yet, we are more than a start, more than an end!
Let our children's children's children's children...
Let our mother's mother's mother's mother...
Let our father's father's father's father...
Let our parents' children's children's children's children...
Let our ancestral parents' parents' parents...
Let Lè' and Njíŋ, nay, the last born of this second...
re-echo our feats, fears and failures up and down
Time's scales of sun and rain within the planets,
be ye, gods or humans!

"Faith of our children holy faith
We will be true to thee till...
Lands of our forbear, unaging lands
We will be true to thee till..." (singing)!

S:- :- f:- :- S:- :- f:- :- S:- :- f:- :-
Tiŋ-ndiŋ   tiŋ-ndiŋ tiŋ ndiŋ
Kiŋ-ŋgiŋ kiŋ- ŋgiŋ kiŋ- ŋgiŋ
Fii-faa   fii-faa   fii- faa
Kuŋ ŋguŋ kuŋ ŋguŋ kuŋ ŋguŋ
Kuŋ ŋguŋ   kuŋ ŋguŋ kuŋ ŋguŋ
Kuŋ ŋguŋ u—u—u....................uŋ! *

* S.O.S. (inaugurated in 1906 as Hauptmann Glauning was in Nsaw)

Rome (1970) Kitiíwúm (1973) Paris 2nd November 1978

EMANCIPATION

I believe
the hub remained behind
in the ground, around the fire-place,
not far from the grindstones
over which our womenfolk worked thirstily
to feed our children!
Yes, around the fire-place
where our youths rebuild guitar-bridges
with the broken calabashes,
wherein, intact, we had fetched
and stored the fresh water
from the streams of our free days;
around the sacred spring-forest
where the militant snakes with silent tread,
dwell and guard and muse
in the silence of sacredness and lore.

So,
amorously human
our anointed memories of echoes
endure in stamina
around our fire-places and whet-stones.
Yet still fleeing away
from their savage deeds
with murmurs of defiance,
aching but never ticking away
with those taximeters of market-days
and crops of slavery, linking us
to lost names, lost tongues
whose relics now grow into pathfinder-tales
of lives of ossified sphinxes
and ship-waters and plantations.

I believe
the hub remained behind
in the slave-songs of shrivelled liberties
we never recapture to scan and sing
until we win.

RUINS

Memories no weather-day should uproot!
a noble reed we inherit to nurse and transmit
intact and free from storms of oblivion!
An overgrowth of shrubs we tend into future years
like an unburnt timeless forest of elephant grass!

Rain-waters our gravity pulls from the heavens
of other eras to bless our soils!
Sanctuaries
we till beyond the congregating valleys
of present fields of eyes and ears
we have taught to know us anew,
though no leopard grows
its colour-straps in old age!

Brains we consult in search of former laws
anticipating new ridges of justice
to sprout and grow and bury us
at best there where we were born,
rather than merely anywhere below the skies!

Legend-names re-echoing lives cropped unripe
into slavery...again
from Hiroshima to Soweto and beyond
with the spittle-drop-arms of shameless discrimination.
Kola trees we abandon unplucked in dismay
inquiring from spiders and egg-pods,
from our *kidív* calabash-portions of rituals
in seasons of want and bloom
amidst dirges of the legacy we began to till
on the eve of their lives.

Ruins!
The tattered music-notes of ages
we still nurse for the incoming,
I salute you!

With the gunshots of our age,
I salute you!
With the hopes and fears of our sowing,
I salute you.

Ruins –
a language community,
heaving with the breath
of festive mànjòŋ voices
we reap and worship and sow
within the sanctuaries of our days
within the sanctuaries of our hills
within the sanctuaries of our heavens
and beyond –
in the name of well-wishers,
I salute you!

I salute you
with the chorus of echoes
you mirror back eternally
through the eaves of time
recalling to build
by dint of love and age and knowledge
sojourns of eras as yet unsurpassed,
renewing unending birth-streams
of passions and love and knowledge and faith
whence waters flow with endowed virginity.

Ruins!
I salute you,
and in search of other better words,
let the drums and xylophone-notes soothe
and embellish the names you bear
from the beginnings of lost but founding ages!

I salute you
whom nature plants in remnants
to resist the flow of waters above and beyond rocks!

You whom generations plant in fields of memory
to resist the winds of age
like rootless rocky reeds;
ye who resisted age
with the mellow jaws of youth,
with the uncooked skin of nature's fruits
with the rough and rude tongues of thunder,
I salute you with the gun-shot voices of our times!

Ruins,
sanctuaries,
unknown to the termite of destruction!
A forest unknown to the moss of oblivion!
I salute and yodel you
through the corridors of a voiceless time
to sparkle and spread
the wisdom of your laws and legacy.

Ruins – our remnants of death!
We salute you
pacing with our steps of discernment –
one-and-two and-two-and-one, one and two....
like our mother-kwí'fòn,
like a bearded father-kìghevshuù, if not a makìbù',
as they pace and betake our steps unto the roads
of luck and evil detection and trampling it to dust
around the premises of our sleep ridden hearths!

Ruins!
We salute you,
as our best remnants of death!

A JOURNEY

Go!
And a child explores its world
Like an arrow through the woods
Piercing through every branch
Conquering the endless fields
To discover its game of gold!
      Come.......!

BAPTISM

News!
more harassing the words
they now convert to harness
into the doings and savings
of injuries and wounds
we notoriously sustain at the noon
of smearing comparisons
we cannot undo
with the rags of sweat-drops of hope
trickling and trickling
into the rivers of their baptism!

Yet, I ask
when or rather for how long?
For how long shall we still look
for a baptism-name outside
the *kwárákwàrà* makings and fibres
of our country – talks?

POST-DISCOVERY

Like you, time's
suckling maiden,
we are now wooed like a river
within a valley's course
into a vision of new clearings,
to grope like aliens out of our times
into the age of post-and re-discoveries
where man , woman and heaven and earth live
on the unrivalled footing of discoveries,
inventing to the rhythm of time and space
but no longer to the rhythm of rivalry,
learning for knowledge rather than for gain
changing names and days, watching stars
not so much to forgive as to take and give,
counting seasons of years not for remembrance
but that the beneficiaries of corrected faults
may implant our age beyond the parasitic age
of our post-discoveries to foster at best
humanity's best ways of her self-education.

A FAMILY TREE

Growth!
Roots
bulky and full
sister-nights
with brother-daylights,
father-weeks
mother-months,
grand-father or grand-mother years
uncles and aunts of seasons
stem from those ledges of centuries,
ancestors won with their sweat -
I'm told all heave
behind my years
ever flowing
with their-wares
around this fig-tree
of a lineage-headwear
which keeps changing foreheads
behind our brother-doors
falling into ruins of memory.

Growth
always moving
from the old to the young!

But why do you,
outgrown ones,
charge us thus in our nakedness
with your powers and mites of missions?

TRICKLES

Trickles
every minute
a drop, a lesson
every minute
a topic
every minute news!
Trickles of leaves
trickles of streams
historical trickles
we bear from within
ruins of water-drops
rulers of a peasant's crop
every hour
a sprouting leaf
every day
a new born baby
every month
a defended script
every year
a page of an age in fashion
in the maker's hands!
Trickles of life
trickles of growth
trickles of rivers
meeting in their *cité*!
Trickles of foot-paths
trickles of lanes and moorings
seasons of suns and rains
scraps of every season
on the laps of every people
tapping *fondoms* behind us!
Tropisms yielding fruits
planting seeds
a sound body bears a disease
as a day bears a night

a child conforms to a parent's wish
parents and children
children and parents!
A river seeks a valley's course
as an eternal shifting cultivation
humanity bears from an eternal harmony –
A beckoning hand to come forth to B
in the liberty of our parental usage
A foot steps out
but soon discovers
no liberty to refuse my liberty
as eyes have seen
hands have touched
ears have heard
once and once only
the cradle-sons of nations yielding
under a ripening sun
drumming the untiring voices of time
within the reins of fashions and powers
in contacts, inventions, projections
and assumptions as trickles
from everywhere.

OUR WAY

Tend it in, boys
Tend it in girls
And lull it
Like children their toys
Rebuilding every broken bit.

Tend it in rhythm
Like a xylophonist his strokes
That hit bit by bit
Into fallen wood from brooks
And move eager crowds
To shake their heads
Clap their hands
Weave their steps
And take their share.

Fend it eagerly
Then poke it duly
Distilling the issuing flames
For
It's your grace
Before your face
It's our gold
Within our fold.

Not even the Gracian Mars can forge
Your gongs
Nor can the 'lunar artisan' carve
Your old doors
Nor he Beatles belittling
Or Händel handling sing
Your songs
Sound
Your drums
And dance
Your dance.

Mungo may meet the Thames
And both shake hands
And wed in the encircling
Depths of the seas; but
Mungo rains fall not on the Thames.

Ours is our culture
Let's soothe Her Wounds
And betroth Her indoors or outdoors
But ever humanly, even in tatters!

Rome, 2nd February 1969

MENTCHEM FALLS

Fresh like the Ba'tum and his attendant Na'tum
from the labyrinth of cross-roads
your pilgrim's fruition sets you anew
into the unique site of this godly sanctuary
with her chasm belchingly awing you into stillness
and you shuffle your feet no more
within these fringed areas of human time.

And in view of her single sliceless laugh
pouring down, shooting over the cliffs unharnessed
into a sacred receptacle of boiling eddies
where she forges breezy mats of sacred smoke
with the head-loads of her prey,
tongue-tied you utter no syllable,
wrapped up as you race with the flow
of her water-clock of laughter
now marking your being.

Waaaaaaaa...........!
She pours and spills and drives out time!

Waaaaaaaa...........!
She nurses awe – the genesis of your worship
and choice of this anvil of our necromancy.

Waaaaaaaa...........!
She quiets the frenzied fauna!

Waaaaaaaa............!
She feeds the sacred fauna and tames the birds
to shun your sight with awry songs of sacredness!

Waaaaaaaa............!
She anoints the shrubs aground!

Waaaaaaaa............!
She graces the heavens with wreath-incense
of smoke begotten from water-depths!
Waaaaaaaa...........The Mentchem spills
and sings with her sediments of legends
away from this abattoir of human tongues
in unison with the hills and lakes above!
Here you review the flow of human time
with the clean eyes of her lakes
the open-arms of her hills now embrace.

Waaaaaaaa........!
Her altar-gongs keep resounding!
The Mentchem laughs over the cliffs,
The Mentchem laughs over the seasons
The Mentchem laughs over time
The Mentchem laughs over memories of time
beyond the lower forests
where neither the Ba'tum nor the Na'tum can defile!

Waaaaaaaa........!
The Mentchem flows on and on
within the guidance of the eyes
of the lakes uphill as she bathes and blackens
rocks and time, irrigating shrubs and groves
with the blessings of seasonal rites
of births and deaths within the fringes
of the life she still spills!

THE HIDDEN VOICE

Its presence!
Its tending hand creeps
everywhere
within the rising moon and sun
within the muttering rain-drops,
maiden-marvels of its making!

In silence it throbs
as each creature drums,
with heels and chords,
its fathomless rhythms
where souls now pace
senseless, rootless, but
thoughtlessly unlocking
to move into a homeless home!

But still
with olive and palm-tree branches
we grace and oil
the silent triumph of a godless age
where to see is to avoid the sight
and to live is to vote and vote
without ever giving the heart
time to pray and bridge the banks
time to love and knot a healthy wedlock.

The rhythms of our age whistle
with the creaking hinges of silent beatings,
heaving beyond the world of marathon grimaces
in which rich lovers and voters
still harness our liberty in the name of money.

THE SEARCH

Still let me spell it
on this palm-frond
as we wait for breezy days
to have their say.
Let me write, speak, chisel and invent
like the ladder of factories lining up
on a sprouting town like you, *O Rühr!*
Let me revive rather than enshrine
my homestead memories
and unravel their knittings
with the skills of our medicine-men,
but avoiding to let loose their germ-talents.

For
mine is a portion of a voluted page,
already written yet in writing,
a word already spoken,
but which we speak
with the language of our age;
wood already chiselled,
yet being chiselled with the chisels
of our inventions and laws;
an invention-stratum on which to build
or plant a fruitful seed still to be sown.
So, let me spell
on this palm-frond
and wait for breezy days
to have their say.

OUR CITY LIFE

Beyond her smiles
I believe
we can unearth living centuries
of culture.

A wayward smile, indeed
on her ebony black lips
beckons to a visiting *Sáŋgó*
waylaying him body and soul
into those market-frames
within our civilization:
dynamism, growth, progress...

No!
"Urbanization"
we chorus and add the refrain.
"Yes Urbanization"
with its evils
"Yes Urbanization"
with its amenities.
"Yes Urbanization"
At all costs?
"Yes Urbanization"
At all costs?
"No! A better Urbanization"
Shiŋgòŋgòn now answers *Titi*.
She has become a high-class *Nyaàŋgó*.
Kimbo', Bamenda, Duwara no longer sell her dresses!
In her latest she blossoms out for a pilgrim *Sáŋgó*
she is *Ledi, Madam, darling, honey...*
Shiŋgòŋgòn smiles to few and rarely too.
Around her there's always a market.

He has a boy.
She has a car.
She has a bar.

Shiŋgòŋgòn serves drinks.
Shiŋgòŋgòn sells drinks to a family of friends:
taxi-drivers, chauffeurs, washer-men, civil servants...
Shiŋgòŋgòn is well-known
she counsels who can help you in need.
There is a tacit agreement within the world around her:
"Consult *Shiŋgòŋgòn* whenever in need."
Her boy receives an extra beer wherever he is recognized,
Her car cannot pass unnoticed.
Her bar is one of the few in town.

Yet her father used to tap palm-wine.
She had moved to K after the events
which ended up sadly for her
because her parents were no more –
father and mother died on the same day
the one in the morning, the other n the evening.
Shiŋgòŋgòn, the city child of her parents
Shiŋgòŋgòn the only pearl of her village
had come to K miserable, sickly and poor;
but a few years in K soon brought her
through and through as an independent somebody.

Beyond her smiles, today
are the memories of fate.

Yet!
Shiŋgòŋgòn intones the rhythms of our city life
with the music of our drums.
Shiŋgŋgòn softens the tunes of our city life
with her speeches – to-day, at *Mr. & Mrs*...
a birthday party speech
to-morrow, at a monthly meeting
she thrills to win the admiration of all.

And days, weeks and years come and go
anchoring their game of festivity
while Shiŋgòŋgòn grows

in fame and belongings
from one to so many bars;
from one to so many cars;
from one to so many boys;
from one to so many names –
The People's Shiŋgòŋgòn!
T.D.B. Shiŋgòŋgòn!
Come -and –see Shiŋgòngòn!
Waka-Waka Shiŋgòŋgòn!
You-do-me-God-go-do-you Shiŋgòŋgòn!
Sabi-all Shiŋgòŋgòn !
Help-me-I-help-you Shiŋgònŋgòn!
Chop-drink-wata Shiŋgòŋgòn!
Maa-Titi Shiŋgòŋgòn!
Maa-boy Shiŋgòŋgòn!
Fashion-and-Nyàŋgá-Shiŋgòŋgòn!

Indeed,
against the sonorous voice
of a church-goer's man of God;
against the left-and-right march
of a school-goer's steps;
against the kà', kà', kà' footfalls,
the German-like military footfalls of *Mr. Sooja*...
against the Salaam Alaikum of Maalam....
against the in-and-out flow from village to town;
against the tempo-strides of our fashions,
Shingongon dresses and irons
her *ŋkùnyà' ŋkuǹyà'* footfalls of modernity
to emerge washed, fresh, cool,
sedgy-sealed, soft-pumpkin-wise
with her varied crowns
of hairstyles and their corresponding hairpins!

With her mirrors of smiles
ear-rings, bangles, golden rings, umbrella, jeans...
gracefully knitted and set up
on those acrobatic high-heels

over which life sprouts her new maiden-leaves
of numerous Saturday T.D.B's
and invites feasting, cry-die, singing...
on everybody's lips....
  Everybody likes Saturday Night
  Saturday Night!
Everybody likes Saturday Night!

Everybody + Everybody!
  Everybody likes Saturday Night!
Everybody + Everybody x Everybody
  Everybody likes Saturday Night!
  Everybody likes Saturday Night!

Everybody + Everybody = Everybody + Nobody!
  Everybody likes Saturday Night!
Everybody + Everybody = Unity
Everybody likes Saturday Night!
Everybody + Everybody = Kintati
Everybody + Everybody = Ujama'a
Everybody likes Saturday Night!
Everybody likes Saturday Night!
Everybody......

Shiŋgòŋgòn, Nyàngá-pikin:
Everybody likes Saturday Night!
Shiŋgòŋgòn, the People's Nyaàngó
Everybody likes Saturday Night!
Shingòŋgòn, the People's Titi:
Everybody likes Saturday Night!
Shiŋgòŋgòn, the People's Ledi:
Everybody likes Saturday Night!
Shiŋgòŋgon, the People's honey:
Everybody likes Saturday Night!
Behind our kwárákwàrà walls
Everybody likes Saturday Night!
With a cup and sooya at hand
Everybody likes Saturday Night!

Till the day breaks
Everybody likes Saturday Night!
Our dreams and hopes
Everybody likes Saturday Night!
Everybody likes Saturday Night!

Beyond her smiles
today
we still unearth living centuries of culture.
Beyond her smiles
we now forge and sow
coming centuries of....
we will crop human failures and feats!

THE ROOTLESS BRANCH

Monday begot Tuesday and we rejoiced
But then, I saw the plants weep
And the dew, the grass dew dripped
And fell with drops of blood.
The blood of our past heroes
Dripped with speed but still
Like ice it cooled the wounds
Of a ravaged mother-earth, the land we love.

We knew the sun would rise
Though on our way from doom,
We judged the tree rejoiced with us
To lose the old to bud the new.

So we plucked the orange -
So we plucked the mango -
So we plucked the guava -
And plucked the palm-tree branches.

And beneath the rootless branches
We sang our songs and lullabies of joy
And soothed our wounds in groups
As we waited for the day of days.

Enugu, Nigeria – May 1967.

CATCHING LIFE

— To Jacques Howlett

Writings –
Those gratings they capture
those gratings they capture for an age-meal
are thoughts on the brink of eternity's oblivion,
crystal-yawns from somewhere
hailing into life – exhaling life
into the life you now tender and want to school
otherwise –
otherwise they escape into the dens of oblivion
and cancel centuried layers of everyone,
inhaling and exhaling nature's best!

Those filings from their ink, minds and pens
Are life breathing and yawning within our veins.

Writings - as crispily fragile
as the unlost leaves of souvenirs,
ridges of tattoos in which our century plants
and treasures in fear of future famines,
but in love and want of future debris!

DISCOVERY

— To Cyprian Kinoti of Uganda

From the sun's rays
Your pen did shine
From a mother's look
Into the horizon of your universal mind!
We discover lately lodes
Of your infant stores of golden thoughts
All is but a souvenir
Past, present and future
All is but a souvenir
The phenomenon of your life
I by-passed the ageless edge of your mind
To settle into its widening caves,
With my hurrah of a discoverer!

A TRIBUTE

— To Dr. Leonard Sùnjò

Rare, a name like yours
that cleanses the fate of misfortune!
Rare, a mind like yours
that delves into healing the body
with a mother-tongue we hardly use well!

With you I share a name
the Nso' as if proverbially, imperatively
or invitingly gave us to pave a way.
With you I share the taste
of cleansing to heal the misfortune
not so much of a sound body as mind
be it distorted, dirtied and soiled in dust!

Sùnjò! With a multitude of well-wishers
Bòngaásu salutes you! In our names of age,
Memories enshrine their old and new testaments

I salute you
Not with the gunshots of our dead! Live long!
Not only with the *wií- wií..lò wán dzòó wán eè!*
or a *bòy fó njò* and the *kèsìn tìnén eè!*
of our mothers and fathers
but with the red feathers of our lore
depicting, unveiling a man of merits
in our midst!

You, a man of patience
You, a man of visions
You, a man of justice
You, a healer by profession
You, a healer by the name you bear!

Today we salute you
we salute you with the echoes
of your deeds!

WISHES

—For Bridgit She'la

If I could see like men of letters
I would translate the chimneys of this city
into the rains over the Mungo.

If I could hear like a tape recorder
I would register the rhythms of this city
into the voice of a drum.

If I could scent like choosy bee
I would like to take back news
about the aroma of its perfumes.

If I could touch like an ancestral mask
I would tell them the discoveries of my hands:
the smoothness of its body! How it glitters like
the body of a snake in broad daylight!
The temperature of its winds goes to school;
the size of its trees doesn't outnumber the boulevards;
the depth of its faith seems measurable
the lopes of its children rise daily
to suit the rhythms of fashion.

If I could sing, the rhythm of this city
will certainly give me notes.
The keyboard will be its local uniformity
woven speculation, faith and fear of faith,
hope and fear of hope, and above all
the taste for gain.

If I could talk with its open parks
how will I console them?
They weep for centuries from constant flogging.
Even, the fear of invasion invites them to cry.
If they were children they would report to their parents

who beats them! Who tramples over their feet
or who snatches their pencils! H'm!

Who tore the chest-pocket of their dáŋcíkí
in an anxiety to make them turn over a new leaf.

How will I tell them that children
elsewhere are dismayed by the messages
of the winds, letters and hearsay?
How will I let them know
that children elsewhere shrug shoulders
even though they envy the aroma of this city's perfumes?
How will I say distance and the fear of distance
wear out the feet of these foreign children
and confine them indoors to copy
what the television may fail to translate?

If I could wear the ancestral mask, I'll certainly school
them
to irrigate their fields with the aroma of the city!
But how will I tell them
that clothes are good for the room and for the waiting-
room;
that trade isn't bad as a means to gain;
that faith throbs in the pockets of our hearts;
that ancestral repute sprang not from a double name,
but from the cloven works of art we chip off and receive?
How? How? How? How? ... How?

OUR WARES

Time!

> Dismantle the saddle of our age
> For us to see

For lies have grown less expensive
> In the world-market
> Of today.

Who buys or who sells
Sssssss————our water-gates!
Point no fingers! Echoes of the times!

Time!

> Unveil the fruits of our age
> For us to see.

Call it fraud, bribery and corruption
Call it lies, prostitution or colonialism
Omnis homo mendax est!

Our times mirror your water-gates!

>   Paris, 1974

THE DESTINY OF GROWTH

Everything downstream!
Everything downhill!
Everything overboard!
So,
comes the echo-shouts
of evil omens
invading the ship-load
of my life
as if once unloaded
I would still survive.

Undo every knot!
Unkey every knob!
Unspin every reel!
So,
comes the echo-shouts
of evil omens
invading me
wishing I were now installed
on the altar of failure.

Yea!
Voices I may still live
to poeticize for an inquiring generation
delving into my years
of planting
of spinning
of storing to harvest,
seasons I would have undone
in order to thrive.

BACK HOME

Back home,
where a brother's contentment fits in
with a sister's surprise
where you rehearse portions of all
in the lap of love's own navel
recapturing and exhaling
news from layers of sibyl-soils and times
construing what the heart, eyes and ears may fail
to feel, see and hear with your presence
hoping to explain more later
unmooring airs
of where-do-you-keep-the-dishes-after-a meal
or measuring the truth of the one taxi's name

Mine Is Yours

in fear of what happens when it all turns out real
believing in the truth of others

God's Will; God's Time Is The Best; Allah....

For
here where a thatched roof ventilates seasons of rains
and a lineage father's call, a mother's whisper
a cousin's voice re-echo a family life
namelessly lived and to be lived in bunches
like banana suckers and fruits sheltering these coffee-
stems.
Here the heavens bless you with their maiden-rains,
the soils maintain you perching
on their termite-feeding moulds,
the air nurses you from moonrise to sunrise
and you forget forests of perforated sorrows exploring
through the unknown of life's victories and funeral songs
over you now smearing and reddening
with the fattening camwood of parental care.

A FAMILY'S CROWN

Let them still hurl the best
of their brickbats
at marketable places
where brother must slander and buy
a brother's name cheaply
or where a sister must hurdle off
a sister's advice to out-grow,
to out-live the disgrace of virtue.
Let them pour in their miasma
of laughter to disown the old-fashioned
and unwarranted choice of the head
that now owns the headwear of the family
tormented, twisted but feared! A new era
within the roofings of an ageless taboo!
Let them sing, yodel or whisper it within
the walls they seal with tête-à-têtes.

Let them trample this headwear underfoot
Or disown the head that now oils it. But...
But God lives in the art of nation building
where, if virtue beams ideally great on all
a fragile headwear soon falls a prey
to the ants of destruction and a faint voice
of the people disturbs a fragile head.

A family headwear rises and falls
with the titles of genuine votes -
a crowning family's headgear like yours,
Oh Ye King and Queen rulers of our lands.

LETTERS TO ETHIOPIA

YAWUNDE

Soils of godly waters,
city of saddles
nursing valleys
shouldering hills
and tethering mirroring homes
of our own naming,
all hail in countless folds!

Who'll stop this pattern of a bird
to allow me survive rather than fly
with your years or with your days
from those springs a noble self
once offered me both in blessing
and in language never to see them dry.

Who'll stop this pattern of a bird
to allow me take shelter
in your forests and gardens
and drink the fresh streams
of your lore of inventions
as your inventions of lore!

City of greenness
City of freshness
City of godly winds
City of camwood maidens
City of unsung names
City-grains of our mustard-seeds
Of the calabash and the iron-leaf
I pray thee to shelter the bones of our tears!

Shelter our father's tears
Shelter our mother's fears
Shelter our children's screams,
Still stirring within our dreams
Over the years like an unweathering rock!

You, the navel-soil of vigilance over
African tongues less in conflict as in peace,
Weathering to unfold dreams of nature's unction
Unrivalled in days as in lands 'no tongue tells'
Nations and continents of incoming generations
Dotting their i's and crossing their t's
Every experience of our *oraural* laws, buttress our soils!

Yawunde buttress the fears and screams of our dreams
And sift out the gravel from the rice
We now have to hand over through a sieve's memory
Unto incoming generations
Night and day,
Day and night everywhere
Every blessed day, week, year and century!

OUR DAYLIGHT

Ethiopia! Ethiopia!
When will you open out
the new pages of your gardens?
I keep nursing you in my dreams
like a farmer tending her seeds
twisting you in my heart, and
re-echoing still
like *Shiŋgòŋgòn* croons her days
with lullabies of our lore
rhyming with the music
of those eye-stripped beads
aging from mother to daughter
beside a wooden bedpost.

Ethiopia!
Already distance dawns
where time plants its clumps of ripening seeds
and I gaze on at each day's horizon without you.

Isolated, but searching, I pray
the winds to do no more than freshen you
the rains to wash and cleanse you
the waves to elevate and preserve you
the sun to brighten you
and leave you wholly mine
for tomorrow's ripening daylight.

EXPECTATIONS

Ethiopia! Ethiopia!
Behold stores of prayers I keep hammering on
the anvil of your name pondering, wondering
why you should leave us seasonal orphans
and crouch over your *shív*-mights
of knowledge, government and faith
as if you had suddenly fallen an easy prey
to an eternal bliss of a choiceless dream,
allowing strange winds to generate and settle storms,
rivers to compete with unrivalled floods
birds and crickets to chirp beyond their fill.

Ethiopia!
It may be one day after this moon of planting,
you will still emerge and break in
whole, fresh, unblemished
as if unfolded from the aeon-shells of nature's egg
to hatch a bird with the wings of daily moon flights,
that sprout with the leaves of an auspicious humanity.

But why crown me with such optimistic thoughts
when the winds have now stopped blowing
over our hills
when the moon no longer appears
in the starless sky of your absence;
when I keep outdoing the rains weeping
over all my tears to rinse and heal
the earth enriched with the ill-gotten wealth
of frailty's craftsmanship: yodelling you
beyond the summit-voices of pests of rivalling storms
still driving me from hillside to hillside.

Ethiopia!
Whoever heralds your dawn
no longer keeps us in suspense.
Whoever heralds your dawn should brandish
a bough for craftsmanship
to meet the forte-wishes of our age.

BENEATH RIPPLES OF WAVES

Ethiopia!
Whispering the same nightmares
flickering with despair
I keep sinking
through the strawless waves
like a ship wrecked out of memory
though still aging in memory
But you evade
like smoke into the heavens
of your sleep
befriending the skies
sending stormy rains
to disarm eyes and arms
I raise
To clutch and fasten
Horizons wrapping up our world.

But
because you alone can now see
my ripple-crown of waves
entombing my hopes
because you alone can still evaporate
all the waves above me
with your sunshine from the skies
and expose me to your heavenly eyes
I will not yield; though now like sheep
within the abattoir of hopes, I will pierce
through the waves to become one with you.

Ethiopia! Ethiopia!
I'm trapped by the waves of weariness
trampling me down into the depths of Zululand.

A FARMER'S DREAM

Ethiopia!
Awake and blossom
like our crops!

In my dreams I walk up and down
through horizons of seasons and lands
marked with sacred palm-fronds of laws
planting seeds, harvesting crops
whither my children's children's eyes
meet their dreams
whither the ears of my grand-great parents
no longer discern the rhythms of our talks
envying and wondering
why maiden-reeds should keep showering
the kisses and comfort of their shadows
upon streams rather than upon our minds
why leaves should keep confiding
to the winds
why rivers should keep flowing away
with their blessings
why birds should keep pursuing the clouds
abandoning the soils
whither lie rations and food-crops
for their days.

Ethiopia!
   Awake and blossom
Through your rains
   Awake and blossom
Through your sunshine
   Awake and blossom
With your children
   Awake and blossom
Ŋkùnyà, Ŋkùnyà!
   Awake and blossom
Nwáyò, Nwáyò!

Awake and blossom
With steady steps
  Awake and blossom
With dignity
  Awake and blossom
Nyaáŋ wùn à nyaáŋ
  Awake and blossom
In peace rather than in pieces
  Awake and blossom
To the hearing of all
  Awake and blossom
As echoes of parental tongues
  Awake and blossom
Like a "motor-driver"
  Awake and blossom
With the telephone
  Awake and blossom
With the television
  Awake and blossom
With the inventions of your age
  Awake and blossom
And so on and so forth
  Awake and blossom!

Ifi naa die O
  Awake and blossom
Ifi naa money O
  Awake and blossom
Ifi naa waka waka O
  Awake and blossom
Ifi naa chop drink wata O
  Awake and blossom
Ifi naa die lif pikin O
  Awake and blossom
Awake and blossom!

A SOLDIER'S SHIELD

Hark!
It's not because
they've succeeded
that I should fail
nor because I've won
that you should give up!

Nay! Courage!
Our dignity now meanders on the verge
while we are soothed to a drowse
in beds of rosy corruption.

Bribery like corruption, believe me,
is culture uprooting itself up-stream;
we cheek it not by quantity or quality
but rather we should nip it in the bud
like a wanton stone in royal cymbals of beads
framed to match and resound with the strength
of their interior making.

Ours to shun and keep clean of its mucus-dung
And catch the termite of a seasoning humanity.

THE ETERNAL TATTOO

Brother hark!
Tiptoeing around the blooming fields
And tethering the reins of our embers
I sow seeds because I'm a crop.

I abandon the laughing crowd
To weave new riddles
Out from the dancing crowd
We fell down the mahogany
To lay out a new xylophone set
We search for leather for a new drum
We survey a new playground for a juvenile dance
Where our embers never grow poor
And our xylophone never wears out.

Fallen wood from untrodden fields
Our xylophone – a ladder bridging every note
It bridges our age to ancestral drummings
We bridge the woods, fallen and unfallen
As heralds of a common lore.
Brother hark!
This is my prophecy:
The tattoo of our lives smoulder on
From the seeds or weeds we sow
From the riddles we weave
From the dry skin that crowns the drum crackles
A crop of our era's craft!
The tattoos of an age never smoulder away!

The blossoming fields like the dancing folks
Are fertile embers with bridles in our hands
I till with the spade of hope lengthening my arms
I sing with the voice of river falls strengthening
My faith in a sprouting Mànjòŋ chorus
Because like you I am a crop!

A NATIVE SONG

With the cue
Below the loft
We took it up to resound
HOLY, Holy, Ho! ...
But with a solemn whetted voice
They slashed it off
Drumming it evenly
And curbing it duly
In a known tongue
As we gaped unto the end.
Then I felt a sacred chill
Slowly blowing in
And hovering over us,
It enveloped us
Within those marble walls
Of our Roman shrine
In the silence that reigned
And on our knees
We scanned the sacred folds
Unfolding the mysterious fold: a renewing plea
To now love with drums and clanging cymbals.

FILINGS

Nothing is lost
Nothing is lost where
silence, forgetfulness and aging hope
survive.

Nothing is lost
from the catalysts of waves
driving our heroes ashore.

Nothing is lost
in what rots off
when crops ripen.

Nothing is lost or forgotten
in a singer's sol-fa
feeding on the decaying notes
of our age.

Nothing is lost or forgotten
in the writer's torn pages
ushered to eternalize in the scrap-paper bins
of our forgetfulness.

Nothing is lost even if forgotten
at each twist of the artist's eye
enriched with continuous sighs of patience
before those choiceless bits of silence
falling off as unruly as unmistaken
to unveil the incoming hero.

Silhouettes rife with the clamorous voices
Of filings, rejected and born to die
I embrace them all with the arms of posterity
Upgrading the rejected and the chosen.

Dreamy still I mutter
Nothing is lost
for a tattooed race issuing
from lost generations;
Let us install their shadows, light and darkness.
Let us eat their grains without devaluing their chaffs.
Let us read the smile of the dahlia and the farmer
sweating within the garden with weeds and crops.

For nothing is lost
even after the harvest
where silence, forgetfulness and aging hope
now survive.

A MOTHER'S LOVE

The value of a mother's love
Is a thing not for a guess
But for mine or your experience
Discovered in its absence.

Like from a spectrum its rays unfold
Her wonderful colours of gold,
When all but her memories remain
Our daily instrument of pain.

In peace we think we are in trouble
So we look around and grumble
When danger comes we tend to cry
For then our thirst for peace begins to rise.

Oh! The value of a mother's love
That fits no foreign glove
When present remains unknown
And comforts us without any frown.

                              Enugu, Nigeria 1965

EARTH

Alive or dead,
how do I know?
far or near or midway,
how do I know?
Deaf, dumb or blind,
How do I know?

Yet, within her
I was born
with her I will die
with her all of us have come
with her many have gone
with her we come
and we go

Yet she thrives
thirsty of the life
she never tastes twice
climbing over a mould of centuries
as potently as prolific and fertile
without fattening
amidst cannons of sounds and silence,
amidst cannons of rainfalls and sunshine
stalactite-cannons breaking through bandages
of winds soothing
the martyring cannons of lightning
cropped from heavenly pollution

Yet,
she thrives with her crispy stalagmite
for endurance until we grow
cannons of dissuasion as if in sympathy
to pollute centuries of endurance
and mount heavenwards
on the oily ladder of calumny and reputation.

TO OUR KNOWN SLAVE

(In Memory of Bun'go alias Robert Shilling of Aberdeen)

I now perch
suspended in the thin air
of discrimination
competing with Eiffel's patterns
refusing to take turns of vigilance
over the tomb of the unknown soldier, I want
to search for the tomb of the known slave
in this sea still rocking
around my neck
with the unevaporated waters of toil
that set passions amuck
where I cry and shout for you, Ethiopia
calling you by those earthen names of slaves
we buried in effigy beyond our bridges.

I cry and shout
for a child we named in memory – *The House Floor!*
bidding caravans of life merchants
to untomb names from lovelessness set amuck
in this sea of passion, discrimination...
Our House Floor! I cry and scream
Resolute to unearth the known slaves.
With an open mouth I yell out for *Nsaàlav ooooo!*
Running away from every colour of forgiveness
Still longing for an impossible forgetfulness.

NEWS FROM YOU

Pilgrim friend!
Your dew-drops of news keep hardening
the spoors of your life as you climb
this tree of temperatures whither silence soothes
the footpath Columbus opened and stained
with our royal blood....

With a fowl at hand for a sacrifice
we wait for the day you trickle through its branches
to water the soils whither lie
the navel-portions of tendrils budding
and whetting the scythes of dry-seasons.

Here your dew drops of news now impromptu
oil and soil our memento captions of dreams in the knitting
behind the palm-fronds of our last handshakes
while illusions haunt and grace
to sow and harvest from their myrrh-seeds of persuasions
on the green banks of the Seine
ever driving her water-sighs away from the thrones
of those bridges – once blackened by your feet
but now schooled to germinate moss as they mutter
as if from a sky of memories: *Elle songe toujours a toi!*

Illusions! The same illusions
yesterday as today, the same illusions!
Elle ne songe jamais à toi!
Hither or thither we fetch and gather
but our faggots of knowledge and life's experience
for incoming eras of the Mànjòŋ youth. And dream!

BEYOND FLOWERS OF WISHES

If water were mine,
I would give you more than any spring.
If days were mine,
I would allow you to live beyond their number.
If air were mine,
I would bid you to inhale your fill of changeless air.
If heaven's sun were mine,
I would lead you through a life of sunshine.
If you were mine,
I would keep you within the silence of earth's bosom
to learn to listen to centuries
of centurying water gurgles
piercing through our landscapes
with their whetstone music of time

But why,
why should we rival springs
why should we outnumber our days
with the unbroken breath of the changeless
why should we only live in the monotony of sunshine
when our lives run a relay-race
between sunshine and rainfall

Men born to live
Men born to walk and remain two-footed
have been taught to live a limping life
on the one-footed succession of rainfalls!
In panic – everywhere from Hiroshima to Vietnam—
In nervousness – looking up with a beggar's eyes
For changeless coins of sunshine.

GROWTH IN NATURE

In this ecstasy I gaze at the rains
rooted deep in the sky
trees shooting out from the ground
winds germinating from the cardinal points
grow into an equilibrium;
the moon, the stars and the sun smile
from their heavenly topography
into the dazzling eyes of nature in movement:
the streams, the rivers and the sea
merge into unison to satisfy
a scientific mind rootless, homeless, baseless
where streams and rivers sleep daily on their beds
and sing in procession into a common home – the sea
with their roots well rooted in their springs.
Out from this ecstasy I find abandoned men and women
Struggling for a home in the trees, in the seas –
they even now walk and talk on as with the moon
but find themselves rootless, homeless at heart
in a space where liberty is still within reach.

THE SUMMONS

The winds are blowing low
Rain-drops in the rainbow sky
We had kept watching
Stormy eddies of thunder and lightning
When sunshine brimmed the sky
The moment reigned, but still
On and on we watched –
Down, down the deep valley swelled
But the Muses of ancestors brood over us;
Our eyes wept and sank into a trance
But ears pricked up to the whispering winds
And still we lay – orphans in sunshine
On a wide flat rock above the turbulent streams
And slept and dreamt – But dreams –
What were dreams to winds?
Friends? No! Message- owners!
Venus dead and Mercury gone asleep
Mars sounds his elephant tusk
In fright of a Mànjòŋ drum whetting its beats!
A summons! A mighty summons
For a sieging whirlwind dance
Where we remain as indifferent as ever before.

YÍDZƏ̆WÙN

Yours is a name that reminds and befits
every age as it absorbs every place
to breathe and reign within the life
that grows, tilting lilies, harvesting honey,
drying waters always and everywhere like the arm
which assaults, quiets and hardens
the voices of growth unto dust.

Yours, a name we call to remind ourselves
at morn, noon or eve to outlive
transient joys when it's time –
when it's time to fetch wood
when it's time to fetch and rehearse a drum
when it's time to fetch and sever
a sacrificial fowl on the unsoiled portions
of a door-step we water with family tears.

Yea! We call out for *Yídzə̆wùn,*
only to harvest the same echoes, written
in a book of a nameless writer, who comes
to help us in a final agony as if from the upper
or lower house-bed where we lie suffering
in a forest of mortal snake-bites, wounds
from hoe-cuts, malaria bites – still mindful
of echoes of news from modern planes above
or ships below, as we attain old, middle and baby age
everywhere, cankerously lowering everyone in flesh
unto dust where she ever reigns no more as a reminder!

Yídzə̆wùn!
Now behold me with my panegyric of name-givers
in a bid to outbid transient joys and sorrows
within the forgetfulness of repetition
and remind ourselves of a name like yours, O death!
Thou must be immortally eternal,
Since nobody ever sets out to conquer thee!
None but futile hands ever invent a gun to shoot thee!

FILES

If files kept me wond'ring,
  thoughts deterred me!
For my files to come through
  Yawunde must sign
Where Bamenda and Duwara
  heckled and undersigned!

In all I spent a poetic while
musing over memories of town-names
and births of a town's cash and rule
like Duwara and Yawunde
but they kept on singing and signing off
with envelopes of excuses and promises
such as we-shall-be-on-again-tomorrow,
listen-to-us-again-tomorrow!
To gain and buy new fiefs of converts
wearing the same hairstyles and bangles
of bribery and corruption in poverty,
the poverty we can neither drive off
nor describe by the riches of the prostitute
as by the widening wealth of the fraudulent!

As you can judge 'a spade is a spade'
only when one minces no words - after all,
nobody shaves somebody's hair in one's absence!
If files kept me wond'ring, thoughts deterred me
where Bamenda and Buya, Duwara and Garuwa
signed for Yawunde to undersign.
Files never freely and truly came through or away
from the prostitution of embezzlement and corruption!

Vèsən wíy yeèle Oò!   What shall we do Oo!
Bóo bvəər asàki Oò!   To outbid the prostitutes Oo!

By signing. Yes by signing!
Let Bamenda and Duwara sign.
Let Buya and Garuwa sign truly and freely
for heaven to duly review the prostitution of fraud
and outbid embezzlement for Yawunde to undersign!
Files will then freely and truly change and flow away
from the prostitution of embezzlement in our world.

LIFE

I call it a road
which I stretch out at every breathing time
I call it a rope with new knots
which I knot still with other new knots
I call it a stream in which I meander
along its valley's course with no scream

I call it my word with its alpha and omega
I call it my minimal sentence
With its subject in place and a predicate's tense
I call it my book with a maker's handwriting

I call her his statue of my own Madonna
I call her my bundle of firewood smouldering
I call her my lock of knitting wool
with which I spin my new yarns in a house
we build with time and space and matter

Life I call you the soil from which plants grow
on which rivers flow
over which winds and storms blow
in which earthen things glow
with their embers of seasonal tints

We call you the knighted kwí'fòn
who roves our moors and heavens
in a bid to undo evil and increase food yields
we call you a spider's web of our Fondom
whose spring-forests never diminish
We call you our expectant lady quietly walking
into a delivery-room ignoring the sex of her offspring

Life! They call you me
when I move on in the ignorance
of what I have lived or how I shall live
still counting and avoiding wounds.
Life, You're invincible to death!

FIREWORKS

I fear, I dread fire
though I sit by the fire
burning fresh corn-cobs
rebuilding seasonal tales
and dreaming of other fireworks
in the dry season.

Fire discriminates against none
fire eats every wood
irrespective of size, origin and rank
in the kingdom of the woods –
Fire eats all
crippled, crooked or crackling wood
Fire is the hungriest of creatures
though He now burns these corn-cobs
with which I warm my fingers rather than freeze
in the middle of the rainy season.

I've seen fire, like every child,
licking my mother's pot
licking our hills, plains and valleys
licking our sacrificial cocks and goats
licking our tray-pots which distinguish
between the witch and the innocent,
with his tongues of an unrivalled craftsman.

Fire discriminates against none
Fire eats every wood:
the dry wood is firewood
the wet wood is firewood
the hard wood is firewood
the soft wood is firewood,
the grass and the leaves and the roots
bleat like sheep and bow to bonfires.
Fireworks oft send showers of sparks,
to incense the sky where thunder dwells
even when they emerge as a volcano.

When I dream of fire I scream
recalling how He ate our palace-roofs,
the last best thatch of our own making!
He turned our *fondoms*
into the frail pages, the crispy leaves
of modernity where we must now build
as if on the ashen lullabies
of the lost names of tongues,
which once resounded the keyboards
of ageless reigns we still telephone
with the xylophone notes
of other ages and lands. Please Lord,
once we still falter and sin, kindly guide
our steps by telephone and open the fireworks
of hell for us to walk out freely into heaven
and remain among your chosen people!

MESSAGES

Oblivious, I walk through
the heart of the rainy season
unaware of the maiden grass and plants
unrivalled in beauty, greenness and nakedness.

In my dreams I see these blades of grass
looking for no lodgings, no clothings
until a farmer's hoe hoists and enshrines them
elsewhere in a bid to crop folds of seeds
for other seasons, baptizing them pagan-weeds.

And I wake amidst messages
I knotted with blades of grass
now wearing their Christian dresses and left behind
for the readers of our times: like you
humans have learned to uproot and bury
our nakedness to give us lodging and clothing!
Later they beweep us in the best of their widow's weeds
like the relatives of these blades of grass
your hoe hoists and enshrines, O gentle farmer!

But what a wedlock of messages!
Whence comes the farmer's hoe, which portions out
our lands into hoed and unhoed soils which I now distil
with this pen and paper for generations to come,
reminding harvesters of blades of weedy grass
gathered into naked oblivion with the arms
of the inquisition before we're baptized.

INSERTIONS

If only my hand could write
what my being breathes forth
with the wholeness of its flesh
with the wholeness of its soul
which nature fittingly inserts
into the lock-crevices
of time and space
within chains of histories
within ligaments of soils
whither my feet tramp up and down
beneath changing horizons now ushering me
into the keyless perpetuity
of unknown eras of other lives.

I'll sing the wholeness of quenched beings
when first they cracked the walls
of human time and space to live
in perpetual kingdoms with no cockcrows!

Incoming beings! Behold my legend
of a legacy I owe you
now posted in yodels
from the time and space and horizons
within which we breathe to break and branch
into new insertions with neither locks nor keys!
To you, I send my wishes of a safe journey
To you, I send my message of a farewell
To have lived is to have borne a triple name,
Mirroring parental and filial roots, perhaps
Like mine – Bòŋaásu Tanla Kíshaàne

A TAXI –DRIVER'S LAWSUIT

Let our warring wills roar no more!
These soil- portions on which we stand
will outlive us but for the measure
of our minds of justice and injustice
in the world of today and tomorrow.

I drive men, women and children in my taxi
yes, children, women and men not wood,
of all works of life and social classes!
One sues but the nation who sues me
for a crime I never committed – my license,
my taxi vignette, relevant papers and documents
have scarcely rounded their honey-moon
of a valid marriage in any land of justice.
Yet, because of her, your girlfriend and prostitute,
you now sue me for them.

Yes, let him sue me for what I never did!
Treachery will pay him on the footpath he follows.
As in a mist one day he will hear a thunder-twang
in a court where nobody wears a uniform, and
lawyers remain invisible but the court opens
its doors solely to the treacherous whom dust outlives
with the harvest of the next season of justice.

We remember what otherwise we forget
that the soils of the hills, the soils of bone-meal valleys
and the soils of fertile plains will outlive our generation
as millions before us. I fear the dust that blinds eyes.
I fear the dust that moulds the cooking-pot and bricks.

I fear the dust in which seeds germinate!
For, it already devoured our living dead,
though today it still remains as hungry as ever!
I fear the soil and the lot of those who never fear her.
I fear the lot of one standing on dust, promising
injustice like you, sir! My taxi is validly new!
Let our warring wills roar no more! Justice speaks!

BEREFT OF MOCKERY

Lily of the Gods,
set up there at the hilltop of desires,
as if to pull the eyes of ambitious lovers
with the gravity of nature's gifts, ever faithful
to your call, you nursed new currents and waves
of sunny smiles with the blessings of rainfalls
into the soils of our memories of days
you first emerged with beauty and grace, fresh
from the creator's chiseling hands, matchless,
and impeccable as our endowment, proportionate
in flesh and sound, our-child-as-our-child-can-be!
Your God-given self was thus bereft of mockery!

Lily of God! We named you, *Bereft of Mockery!*
We hailed you then with the soup-dish of our red oil,
fattening the very blood within your veins,
singing lullabies in the right vein and whispering
our choicest wills and testaments to you in whistles
of dreams and knowledge within our shortening days
in the hope that one day as a seedling you might....
But today to our dismay, O our Lily of God,
God as we see in the lower or in the upper forests,
Our forested God of the ruined and falling homes,
it's you bequeathing us with your will and testament!
The soup-dish of your premature teething and children,
where nobody discerns our jargon in tears and fears
now season but the red-soil of the epitaph of memories
in a world still aging on the fringes of human suspicions!

Lily of God! Yours, the absence that remains present!
You're the silence that speaks to the guilty!
Lily of God! Our God-given Lily! Set up there or down here,
as above our heads as below our feet, You're bereft of mockery!
Behold our soil portion of a farewell until we take our turns!

GLOSSARY

- Cíkàŋ: (Chikang) A lineage dance of the Védo'ó people among the Nso' of Cameroon. It is often referred to as Shív-Védo'ó, meaning "A medicinal vital talent of the Védo'ó" One of its distinctive marks is that it does not accept gifts of animals in general. Its gifts include salt, oil, groundnuts, kola nuts, camwood, etc. It is a dance under the auspices of women.

- Coŋ: (Chong) A women's club and dance among the Nso'

- Dáŋcíkí (Dangchiki): A Hausa borrowed word for a kind of dress with that name in Lam Nso'.

- *Elle songe toujours à toi*: French for the English, 'She is always thinking of you'

- *Elle ne songe jamais à toi*: French for the English, 'She is never thinking of you'

- Faáy: A title name for some lineage heads among the Nso'.

- Fee: Sound of a flute.

- Fon: Title name of the highest royal ruler and leader of the Nso'

- Fondom: A realm ruled by a Fon.

- Geegee: A name of one of the days of a Nso' eight-day week.

- Ji á wáa yu: A greeting formula among the Nso'.

- Kaáví: A name of one of the days of a Nso' eight-day week.

- Kighevshuù: A mask reputed among the Nso' for detecting evil. A leader of a dance and masks known as Ŋgàŋ, which display at traditional funeral celebrations.

- Kɪkéŋ (Kikeng, Ŋkèŋ): Popularly known as a peace plant, it is a perennial plant that grows around sacred places among the Nso'.

- Kìŋgìŋ (Kinging): A solemn sound of a big bell.

- Kiloòvə̀y: A name of one of the days of a Nso' eight-day week.

- Kùŋgùŋ (kungung): A sound of wooden gongs.

- Kwàŋkwàŋ (kwangkwang): A type of bow used formerly by the Nso'.

- Kwí'fòn (kwifon, kwihfon): It often depicts an affectionate or dignifying name, an inner circle of the ŋwéròŋ or ŋwéròŋ itself among the Nso'.

- Lè': A founder ancestral name in Nso' history and mythology.

- Makibu': A male lineage dance and mask of the Vedo'o of the Do' Run lineage in Kitiiwum, Nso'.

- Mànjòŋ (Manjong): A men's club and society similar to the women's Coŋ (Chong).

- Ndiŋ (Nding): Sound of a musical instrument.

- Ŋgaà Mbom: God as the Creator or owner of the created as the one who created them once and for all.

- Ŋgaà Mbóm: The owner of creating, making. The person creating, the maker of all. Its synonyms are Nyùy Mbóm, Taà Mbóm. In Nso' classical thinking, God is Nyùy Mbóm, Ŋgaà Mbóm, Taà Mbóm, or God as the inspirational source of continuous creativity.

- Ŋgàŋ (Ngang): One of the most ancient mask-dances among the Nso'

- Ŋgày wìr (Ngaywir): An elder's generic name in Lam Nso'.

- Ŋgírì (Ngiri): A palace-mask society and dance, similar to the ŋwéròŋ, its twin society among the Nso'.

- Njíŋ (Njing): A founder and ancestral name in Nso' history and mythology

- Ŋwéròŋ (Ngwerong): A palace-mask society and dance. It maintains peace and order. It is also often referred to as Shív Nsay, unlike its twin society known as Ŋgírì among the Nso'.

- Ŋgòylùm: A name of one of the Nso' eight-day week.

- Ŋkùnyà': Slow but fashionable gait in walking. Often used in Pidgin English.

- Nsəə̀rí: A name of one of the Nso' eight-day week.

- Ntàŋrìn: A name of one of the Nso' eight-day week.

- Nwayo: Its multiple meaning includes caution, precaution, 'with care', 'attentive,' almost the equivalent of the German *'vorsichttig'*. A common linguistic coin between Nigeria and Cameroon, the word itself most probably originates from the Igbo language.

- Nyaáŋ: Lam Nso' word for peace.

- Nyaàŋgo (Nyaango): It means a maiden, a lady of middle age. It is one of the common linguistic coins circulating in Cameroon.

- Nyùy Mbom : God, Creator

- Nyùy Mbóm: God of creating, making or God as maker

- Rəə́vəy: A name of one of the days of a Nso' eight-day week.

- Saŋgo (Sango): A gentleman. It is also like Nyaaŋgo one of the common linguistic coins in Cameroon.
- Sáar: Sorghum or a millet like crop grown formerly by the Nso' who announced its harvest publicly.

- Shív: A talent or genius with medicinal undertones.

- Shikùmkùm Koó: A mark of success piecemeal

- Taàmànjòŋ (Taamanjoŋ): A Mànjòŋ leader. A title name.

- Taà Mbom: Father of the created

- Taà Mbóm: God as the Maker used by the Nso' non-Church goers or home keepers. The title of God as the creating power.

- Taà Mfu': A Mfu' leader. A title name.

- Taà Ŋgwà': Leader of the Ŋgwà', a hunting youth club. It is also a title name. It should not be confused with Taà Ŋgwá', the leader of any kind of organization.

- Taà Nto': A title name.

- Taà Wòŋ: A title name.

- Taà Wónlè: A title name that one finds in the course of the Nso' tradition of renaming family members. Like its twin name of Yeè Wonle, it is given to the officiating priest and priestess of the ceremony of renaming.

- Tìndìŋ (Tinding): Sound of a drum

- Tíŋekárí (Tikar / Tikari): A collective name regrouping many fondoms in the Grassfields of Cameroon. Lam Nso' suggests its derivation from Tíŋ (Ting) e kárí: The stock revolves or moves around.

- Védo'ó: A Nso' clan. Védo'ó are divided into three main branches of Do' Run, Nsə' and Do' Ŋgvən lineages.

- Vibìŋ veé yuv (Vibing vee yuv): Doves from the heavens.

- Vilùŋ veé nsay (Vilung vee nsay): Earthly kites

- Wà'bìn: A collective name for the youth in Lam Nso'.

- Wáylùn: A name of one of the days of the Nso' eight-day week.

- Yeèwòŋ or Yeè Woŋ (Yeewong): A title of the Queen Mother.

- Yeè Wónlè: A priestess officiating during the name-giving ceremony when members of a family acquire new names.

- Yídzə̀(é)wùn: Death subsists in the body.